NFL ★ TODAY

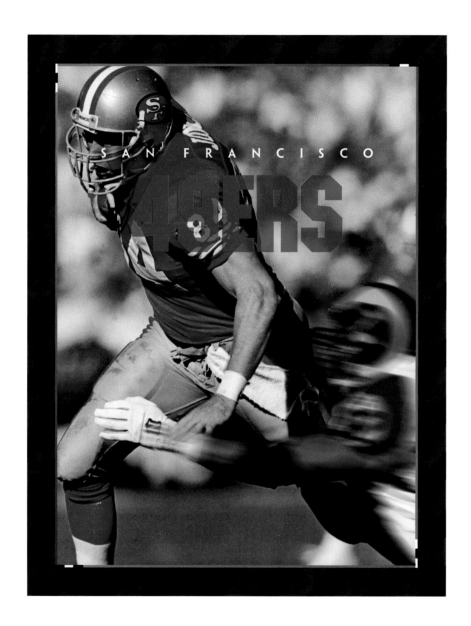

SAN FRANCISCO 49ERS

LOREN STANLEY

CREATIVE ♥ EDUCATION

Published by Creative Education
123 South Broad Street, Mankato, Minnesota 56001
Creative Education is an imprint of The Creative Company

Designed by Rita Marshall
Cover illustration by Rob Day

Photos by: Allsport Photography, Bettmann Archive, David Madison,
Duomo, Fotosport, and SportsChrome.

Library of Congress Cataloging-in-Publication Data

Stanley, Loren, 1951-
San Francisco 49ers / by Loren Stanley.
p. cm. — (NFL Today)
Summary: Traces the history of the team from its beginnings through 1996.
ISBN 0-88682-786-8

1. San Francisco 49ers (Football team)—History—Juvenile literature.
[1. San Francisco 49ers (Football team) 2. Football—History.]
I. Title. II. Series.
GV956.S3S83 1996   96-15221
796.332'64'0979461—dc20

123456

For many Americans, San Francisco is a city of mystery and romance. A popular spot for vacationers and honeymoon couples, this Pacific coast city offers such sights and sounds as a breathtaking view of the Pacific Ocean and the clang of trolley car bells. Fishermen's Wharf, the Barbary Coast, and the Golden Gate Bridge are well-known landmarks in this city, one of America's most beautiful. The San Francisco 49ers are also a landmark of sorts, for San Francisco was the first city west of the Rocky Mountains to be given a professional football franchise.

It all began in 1946, when the new All-America Football

Dana Stubblefield was the sack leader in the 1990s.

Speedy Len Eshmont averaged over twenty-six yards on kick-off returns for San Francisco.

Conference established a club in San Francisco. Two brothers, Tony and Vic Morabito, had founded the team because they knew that the people of their hometown wanted a pro sports franchise. The Morabito brothers, whose motto was "go first class or not at all," had worked hard to establish a football team in the Bay area. Led primarily by Tony, their hard work paid off as the team prospered in its first three seasons in the AAFC.

Although the team was doing well, the All-America Football Conference was not, and in 1949 the league folded. Luckily for Tony Morabito, the National Football League offered to let four AAFC franchises enter the NFL. One of those teams was the San Francisco 49ers, named for the gold seekers who settled around San Francisco in 1849 during the California gold rush. Tony Morabito hired a new staff and began looking for players to open the 1950 NFL season. He intended to make the 49ers a winning team for his beloved San Francisco.

A SUCCESSFUL BEGINNING

The 49ers' first coach in the NFL, Lawrence "Buck" Shaw, was put in charge of recruiting the talent that would fill the team's roster. Many of the players were men the NFL had cut because they were considered too old or not talented enough to play for the established teams. Buck Shaw set out to surprise his fellow coaches by molding these players into a winning squad. He was a stunning success.

One of Shaw's first choices for the new 49ers was a small, wiry quarterback, left-hander Frankie Albert. Albert, only 5'8", joined the team in 1950. After playing with the 49ers, he later returned to coach the team (1956-1958). Albert's backup

Bryant Young (#97) was Defensive Rookie of the Year in 1994 (page 7).

quarterback in his first year was Yelberton Abraham Tittle, better known as Y.A. Tittle.

Tittle had played for the old AAFC Baltimore Colts and had been searching for a new team since the AAFC crumbled. Shaw signed him in 1950. Tittle, who emerged as a standout quarterback with the 49ers and the New York Giants, became famous for his "Alley Oop" pass to R.C. Owens under the goal posts. As one newspaperman said, "It's the strangest thing I've ever seen on a football field." Owens, a former basketball star, would gauge Tittle's throw, jump as high as he needed to bring down the pass, and land in the end zone for a touchdown. The tactics were definitely unorthodox, but they did work.

Shaw also signed Hugh McElhenny, who joined the team in 1952. Known as "the King," McElhenny got his nickname during his first game in a 49ers uniform. On the initial play of the game, McElhenny took the ball and ran 60 yards. Coach Shaw, not recognizing the play that McElhenny had just run, called Frankie Albert off to the sidelines. Albert told the coach that McElhenny had refused to carry the ball unless he could have a play created just for him. "He's the king," Albert told Shaw. "McElhenny is the king of runners." The nickname stuck.

But McElhenny wasn't the only star in the San Francisco backfield with a catchy nickname. Shaw also snagged Joe "the Jet" Perry, who ran for over 1,000 yards in 1953 and 1954 and scored an astounding 50 rushing touchdowns. Perry was given his nickname for his fast feet and his ability to break free of blockers. With talent such as McElhenny and Perry, San Francisco put together six straight winning seasons between 1951 and 1956.

The 1957 season was again a winning one. Unfortunately, it ended on an unhappy note. At halftime of a Chicago Bears-49ers game, the last contest of the season, the 49ers entered

1 9 5 2

Y.A. Tittle's talents began to blossom as he passed for over 1,400 yards during the season.

their dressing room behind 17-7. At that same time, team president Tony Morabito, who had been watching the game, died of a heart attack. The players, shocked at hearing of Morabito's death, went back out on the field with feelings of anger and sorrow, determined to win the game in memory of their owner. They did, by a score of 21-17. But, unfortunately, this fervor didn't carry over into the playoffs, where a dazed 49ers team blew a 27-7 lead over Detroit to lose 31-27.

Tough guy! Defensive tackle Leo Nomellini made his sixth consecutive Pro Bowl appearance.

A CHANGE OF FORTUNE

The 49ers had managed to scratch out some success in their earlier years, but the period between 1959 and 1967 was a frustrating one. Although they consistently ended up with either winning seasons or a .500 record, they rarely finished higher than third or fourth place in the NFL Western Division. Head coach Red Hickey (1959-1963) and Jack Christiansen (1963-1967) had fine players, but they could not manage to get them to the top.

One of these fine players was John Brodie. The talented quarterback came to San Francisco in 1957 from Stanford University in the college draft. He stayed with the club until 1973. By the time he left, he had led the league in various years in passing completions, yardage and touchdowns and had won the Most Valuable Player award in 1970. Brodie remained in San Francisco even though other teams tempted him frequently with promises of higher salaries. As 49ers' front office manager Lou Spadia remembered, "Brodie was the only football player I knew, or know of, who didn't allow money to interfere with his attitude toward the game or his performance."

Brodie was also aided by a defensive line that knew what it

Fullback William Floyd was an offensive force in the 1990s (pages 10-11).

Quarterback John Brodie had a banner year, passing for 3,020 yards and 22 touchdowns.

meant to scramble up an opponent's game plan. Charlie Krueger, who played defensive tackle with the 49ers, came to the team as one of its early draft picks and stayed for 15 years. Krueger was known as one of the most scrupulous men in pro football. When Lou Spadia tried to pressure the young Texas A & M star to sign a pro contract before college graduation, Krueger refused, insisting that he had promised not to sign any contracts before his team played in the Gator Bowl.

Honesty and raw talent aside, the San Francisco 49ers did not have the assets necessary for real success. Although they had winning seasons and played the occasional great game, something was still missing.

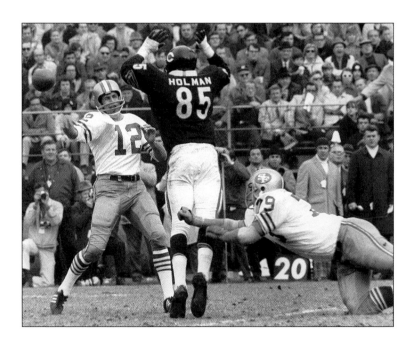

D ick Nolan, the quiet, wiry Irishman, already had a long list of champions on his resume when he came to the 49ers. A defensive back during his college days at the University of Maryland, Nolan graduated in 1953 and signed up with pro football's New York Giants. From 1953 to 1961 he played for New York and for the Chicago Cardinals. When he decided to retire from playing in 1961, his old friend Tom Landry, then coach of the Dallas Cowboys, asked Nolan to join him in shaping his young team. Nolan accepted Landry's offer and remained with the Cowboys until 1967, when he left to become head coach of the 49ers.

Rookie Gene Washington was one of the club's top receivers with thirty-three catches during the season.

Under Nolan, the 49ers gradually climbed from the bottom of the standings to divisional champion. Offensively, a lot of the credit went to Brodie. He sparked a San Francisco offense which was one of the highest scoring in the league. Supporting his efforts were the dynamic wide receiver Gene Washington, the dependable tight end Ted Kwalick, and the durable running back Ken Willard.

Coach Nolan's passion, however, was defense. He worked feverishly to develop young but talented players. Among these skilled defenders were Cedrick Hardman, Dave Wilcox and Bruce Taylor. For experience and savvy, Nolan turned to veteran defensive back Jimmy Johnson.

Drafted from UCLA in the first round in 1961, Johnson would be a member of the team until 1976. In a career that spanned 16 seasons, Johnson had 47 career interceptions and returned them for nearly 615 yards. For his accomplishments, Johnson was honored by being named All-Pro four times. An athlete

Cornerback Jimmy Johnson led the 49ers with four interceptions and was a fearsome pass defender.

who was capable of playing any number of positions, Johnson played wide receiver in 1962 and cornerback in 1963. In 1971 he played three games with a broken wrist, evidence of his dedication to the game and to his team.

Despite all of their talent, the San Francisco 49ers were still unable to win consistently during Dick Nolan's tenure. Winning seasons in 1968, 1970, 1971 and 1972 were interspersed with losing efforts in 1969, 1973, 1974 and 1975. Victory always seemed within the reach of Nolan's team, only to be snatched out of their hands.

A good example of this was the thriller played on December 23, 1972, when the 49ers met Tom Landry's Dallas Cowboys in the NFC division playoffs. The fourth quarter began with Dallas behind 28-13. In an effort to spark his team, Landry replaced quarterback Craig Morton with Roger Staubach, one of the game's best performers under pressure. True to his reputation, Staubach led the Cowboys to 14 points in less than two minutes. The Cowboys ultimately won 30-28, destroying the 49ers' dreams of a Super Bowl. Although the 49ers got their revenge in a last minute 28-27 win over the Cowboys in the 1981 NFC championship game, Dick Nolan would not be there to witness it. The 1972 defeat symbolized Nolan's inability to turn his team around. What would it take to make San Francisco a consistent winner? That question weighed heavily on the minds of many San Francisco fans when Dick Nolan left the club in 1975.

STARTING OVER

I n 1977, the Morabito family made it known that they were interested in selling the 49ers. Enter Edward DeBartolo Jr.,

Defensive end Cedrick Hardman (#86) racked up 15 sacks in 1975.   15

Under Bill Walsh's guidance, the 49ers tripled their number of victories from 1979.

the son of a Youngstown, Ohio family that had made millions building shopping malls around America. The DeBartolos and their fellow investors raised the $17-million asking price for the club and bought it that same year. DeBartolo then announced to the press that he liked to win and that he intended to do whatever was needed to make his team into a winner.

All the enthusiasm in the world, however, couldn't turn the 49ers around in 1978 and 1979. Two consecutive 2-14 seasons, and four coaches in three years, convinced DeBartolo that drastic changes needed to be made in his game plan.

The fifth coach DeBartolo hired was just the medicine the hurting team needed. Bill Walsh, a man who had never played pro football and looked more like the college professor he was than a coach, took the reins of the team in 1979. Walsh did have coaching experience with several pro teams. In 1966, Walsh had been an assistant at Oakland. He held the same position with the Cincinnati Bengals from 1967 to 1975. When Bengals' coach Paul Brown retired in 1975, Walsh expected to be named as his successor. When someone else was chosen, Walsh was devastated. Not only had Walsh not gotten the head coaching job, but Brown had also gone to great lengths to make sure that his popular former assistant couldn't find a head coaching job anywhere in the pros.

As a result, Walsh coached at Stanford in 1977 and 1978, winning two bowl games in a row. When DeBartolo called and offered him the head coaching position in San Francisco, Walsh accepted at once. As the next ten years proved, DeBartolo was a very good judge of coaching talent; Walsh became one of the game's most brilliant practitioners.

Quarterback Guy Benjamin, one of the players Walsh

Wide receiver Dwight Clark was a magnet for passes. 17

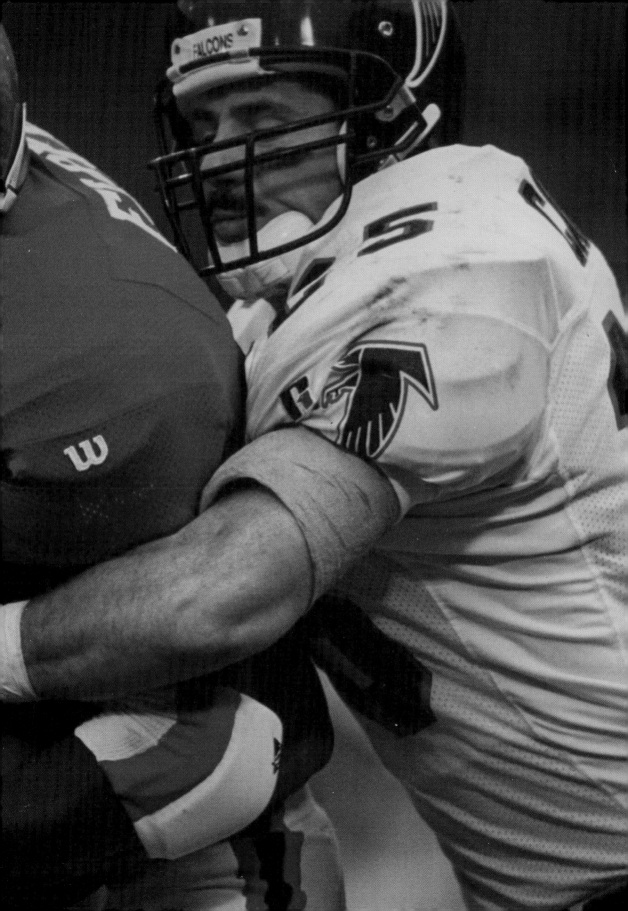

Defensive end Fred Dean made 17.5 sacks.

brought up through the ranks, described Walsh's unique approach to football when he said, "With Bill, instead of pointing around and telling you what to do every time, he shows you once and expects you to understand it. He allows you to surround yourself with an air of responsibility." Just like the good teacher he had been in the classroom, Walsh was a good instructor on the field.

But the fact that the 49ers had spent two years in the NFC cellar gave doubts even to the usually optimistic Walsh. "I'll be honest with you," he told reporters. "Turning this team around will be no easy matter. It's going to take time."

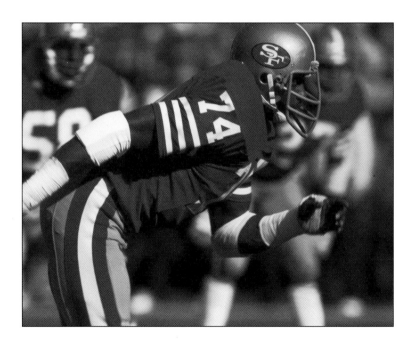

he turnaround would happen much quicker than anyone could have anticipated. Within three short years Walsh's 49ers would go from the bottom of the standings to Super Bowl champions. How could such a dramatic improvement be possible?

Walsh's sharp eye for talent brought many new faces and skilled players to San Francisco. Dwight Clark, Ronnie Lott, Keena Turner, Eric Wright and others came via the college draft. Jack Reynolds and Fred Dean were acquired through key trades. Together they equalled success. But much of the credit was due to a young quarterback from Notre Dame.

Record setter! Roger Craig broke the 49ers' single season rushing record with 1,500 yards.

Joe Montana was born in Monogahela, Pennsylvania, an area that produced other great quarterbacks such as George Blanda, Johnny Unitas, and Joe Namath. As a child, Montana showed a special aptitude for sports. He loved to play football and baseball. In fact, he was such a good baseball prospect that North Carolina offered him a baseball scholarship. However, he was equally talented in football, and it was his first love.

At his parents' urging, he decided to attend Notre Dame, home of the Fighting Irish. When Montana showed up for freshman practice, he found that the world of college football was quite different from that of high school. Instead of being the star, he was merely a seventh-string quarterback. He saw little play during his first year. As a sophomore, however, Montana was put into a crucial game against North Carolina. With only 62 seconds left on the clock, Montana completed four passes for 129 yards and 15 points, clinching the game for the Irish. This

Quarterback Joe Montana was a consistent record-breaker.

was the first of many astonishing saves Montana recorded at Notre Dame. In his final college game, the 1979 Cotton Bowl against the University of Houston, Houston led 34-13 in the third quarter. In what seemed like a miracle, Montana ran, passed, and fought his way to a 35-34 victory in the last two seconds of the game.

Many NFL coaches, however, thought that this college standout was too small for the pros. Not selected until the third round of the draft by San Francisco, Montana set out to prove his critics wrong. And it didn't take long.

During his 14 years with the 49ers, Montana established himself as more than a premier quarterback. He became "Joe Cool," a living legend renowned for his ability to perform at his best when the game meant the most. Montana led San Francisco to four Super Bowl victories—in 1982 over Cincinnati (26-21), in 1985 over Miami (36-18), in 1988 over Cincinnati again (20-16), and then in 1989 over Denver (55-10). The final two triumphs enabled the 49ers to join the Pittsburgh Steelers as the only teams in NFL history to win back-to-back Super Bowls.

Along the way, Montana made some personal NFL history of his own. He became the only player ever to be named the Most Valuable Player in the Super Bowl three times. He also won the regular season Most Valuable Player award in 1989 and 1990. By the end of his career, Montana ranked amongst the top five NFL quarterbacks of all time in the key categories of passing yards, completions, and touchdown passes.

"He's the kingpin, the reason we've been able to maintain this," remarked safety Ronnie Lott, an All-Pro who is considered by many to be the best at his position in NFL history. Head coach George Seifert, who took over for Walsh after his resignation in 1989, agreed, "You look at him from the sidelines, and you're almost in awe. He's always been our leader."

Perennial All-Pro cornerback Ronnie Lott led the 49ers with five interceptions.

Left to right: John Taylor, Keena Turner, Jerry Rice, Ronnie Lott.

Montana led the 49ers, but no one individual can win four Super Bowls. DeBartolo, Walsh, Seifert and company surrounded their quarterback with exceptional players: Roger Craig, Jerry Rice, Don Griffin, Tom Rathman, John Taylor. . . the list goes on and on.

It was a group of skilled athletes, however, that was willing to sacrifice for the good of the team. "Sure we have some great individual players," commented All-Pro wide receiver Jerry Rice, "but so do many other teams. What we have that is unique, is a collective desire to be the best football team ever."

Rice himself was a perfect example of the blending of individual greatness with the 49ers team concept. A number one draft pick out of Mississippi Valley State in 1985, Rice quickly established himself as a major star by winning the league's Most Valuable Player Award in 1987. He went on to break every major NFL career receiving record and to become—during his playing days—the consensus choice as the greatest wide receiver in NFL history. Yet Rice never clamored for attention and was always happy to give praise to his teammates.

1 9 9 0

Defensive end Charles Haley led the 49ers with 16 sacks and was an All-Pro.

A NEW ERA AT QUARTERBACK

Rice and his fellow 49ers faced a new kind of challenge in 1991. The aging Montana suffered an elbow injury and was out for the entire season; he would ultimately be traded to the Kansas City Chiefs. Clearly, it was time for a new quarterback to take the reins in San Francisco. But who could possibly replace Montana?

Steve Young had served as a back-up to Montana for four years. Young had begun his NFL career with the Tampa Bay

Defensive tackle Bryant Young takes down a Charger (pages 26-27).

J.J. Stokes' 39-inch vertical leap allowed him to receive long passes.

Buccaneers in 1985, and with both the Bucs and the 49ers he had shown flashes of potential greatness. But the San Francisco fans—accustomed to the brilliance of Montana—were skeptical about their new quarterback.

Young lost little time in winning them over. In 1991, he led the NFL in passing efficiency with a 101.8 quarterback rating. The 49ers failed to make the playoffs, but Young had arrived. The next year he became the NFL's Most Valuable Player and started for the NFC in the Pro Bowl. Young was the Most Valuable Player again in 1994 and led the league in passing efficiency for the fourth straight year, breaking the former record of Montana with an all-time high rating of 112.8.

But one key accomplishment was still missing from Young's resume: a Super Bowl victory. The 49ers helped to fill in that gap by signing free agent cornerback Deion Sanders. Nicknamed "Prime Time," the flashy Sanders grabbed six interceptions—three of which he returned for touchdowns—during the 1994 season. Sanders won the NFL Defensive Player of the Year award for his heroics.

With Young leading the offense and Sanders sparking the defense, San Francisco was ready for a memorable post-season. After having lost to Dallas in two straight NFC championship games, the 49ers bested the Cowboys 38-28 in the 1994 title game. It was on to the Super Bowl—where the 49ers trounced the San Diego Chargers 49-26. Young set a Super Bowl record with six touchdown passes—surpassing the old mark of five by Montana—and was named the game's Most Valuable Player. A jubilant Young, who had often been unfavorably compared to Montana (because of his failure to win an NFL title), now told the media: "I've got the monkey off my back at last." As for the 49ers franchise, it won its fifth Super Bowl—tying it with

Star quarterback Steve Young could run as well as pass.

Jerry Rice was a Pro Bowler for ten straight seasons.

Linebacker Ken Norton Jr. added defensive muscle in the 1990s.

Chris Doleman brings his pass rushing expertise to the 49ers.

Dallas (which won its fifth Super Bowl in 1995) for the most Super Bowl victories by any NFL team.

An injury to Young and the departure of Sanders to the archrival Cowboys slowed down the 49ers in 1995. By the standards of most clubs, they enjoyed an exceptional year, winning the NFC Western Division with an 11-5 record. But a first-round playoff loss to the Green Bay Packers put a sour note to the end of the season.

The 49ers are an experienced championship club. They are never satisfied with what they have already accomplished. As Joe Montana once put it, "Every Super Bowl becomes more precious. The more the merrier." Don't be surprised if the 49ers add to their stellar Super Bowl legacy in the years to come.